JAN 0 4 2006

E. B. WHITE

Mitchell Lane
PUBLISHERS
P.O. Box 196
Hockessin, Delaware 19707

Titles in the Series

CLASSIC
StoryTellers

E. B. WHITE

by Rebecca Thatcher Murcia

Printing   1   2   3   4   5   6   7   8
Library of Congress Cataloging-in-Publication Data

Murcia, Rebecca Thatcher, 1962 -
        E. B. White / Rebecca Thatcher Murcia.
            p. cm. — (Classic Storytellers)
        Includes bibliographical references (p.) and index.
        Contents: Baby spiders on the dresser — A writer's beginnings — The struggles of a young writer — Finding success in New York City — The inspiration for Stuart Little.
        ISBN 1-58415-273-7 (lib. bdg.)
        1. White, E. B. (Elwyn Brooks), 1899 — Juvenile Literature. 2. Authors, American 20th Century — Biography — Juvenile Literature. [1. White, E. B. (Elwyn Brooks), 1899 — 2. Authors, American. 3. Authorship.] I. Title. II. Series.
        PS3545.H5187z78 2004
        818'. 5209—dc22

                                                                                2003024335

ABOUT THE AUTHOR: Rebecca Thatcher Murcia graduated from the University of Massachusetts at Amherst in 1986 and worked as a newspaper reporter in Texas for 12 years. She is a writer, soccer coach and some-time Spanish teacher in Akron, Pennsylvania. Upon receiving this assignment, Murcia dusted off the same 1952 copy of *Charlotte's Web* her mother had read to her when she was a child. She enjoyed reading the book to her own sons, who are seven and nine.

PHOTO CREDITS: Cover, pp. 1, 4, 6 Hulton/Archive; pp. 10, 16, 20, 26, 30, 36 Division of Rare and Manuscript Collections, Cornell University Library

PUBLISHER'S NOTE: This story is based on the author's extensive research, which she believes to be accurate. Documentation of such research is contained on page 46.

The internet sites referenced herein were active as of the publication date. Due to the fleeting nature of some web sites, we cannot guarantee they will all be active when you are reading this book.

Contents

E. B. WHITE

by Rebecca Thatcher Murcia

*For Your Information

StoryTellers StoryTellers StoryTellers StoryTellers StoryTellers StoryTellers StoryTellers StoryTellers

E.B. White was a poet, essayist, novelist and commentator. He is most famous as the author of *Stuart Little*, *Charlotte's Web*, and *The Trumpet of the Swan*. But he also published books of essays, poetry and letters. He accomplished much in his life as a writer, but he never saw himself as a literary star, once joking that his intellect was better suited to farming.

Chapter 1

BABY SPIDERS ON THE DRESSER

It wasn't a scene that most people would want to find in their bedroom. Tiny baby spiders crawled out of a candy box on the dresser. They strung little spider lines from the hairbrush to the comb, and from the comb to the mirror. From the mirror they rappelled down to a pair of nail scissors.

But to E.B. White, the scene was thrilling. It was about 1950, and he was working on *Charlotte's Web*, one of his most famous children's stories. He had carefully watched while a spider in his barn in Maine had laid eggs in an egg sac. When he had to travel to New York City, he put the mother spider and the egg sac in the candy box. In his apartment in New York, he put the box on the dresser. Soon the baby spiders were born and made themselves at home. White was pleased. His cleaning staff wasn't.

"We all lived together happily for a couple of weeks," White wrote later. "And then somebody whose duty it was to dust my dresser balked, and I broke up the show."[1]

Chapter 1 BABY SPIDERS ON THE DRESSER

By then he had what he wanted. *Charlotte's Web*, like White's other children's books, has an unlikely story line that came from his active imagination. It is about a barn spider named Charlotte who is trying to save the life of a pig. The animals in *Charlotte's Web* talk to each other. Fern, an eight-year-old girl, easily understands what they say.

However, White wanted to make sure that his book was also based on reality. That meant that the description of Charlotte's weaving and laying eggs had to be accurate. Both on his farm and in his apartment, he studied spiders and learned as much as he could about their web-making techniques and life cycle.

White used the same wonderful mixture of fantasy and fact in all his books. It was surely one of the keys to the marvelous success of *Charlotte's Web*, as well as *Stuart Little* and *The Trumpet of the Swan*. All three books include stories that are impossible in the "real world." A spider writes words in her web. A swan plays the trumpet. A human mother gives birth to a mouse-like child. And yet White filled them with wit and wisdom that has made them treasured classics.

FYInfo

Senator Joseph R. McCarthy

Senator McCarthy

In 1950, the most important newsmaker was Senator Joseph R. McCarthy. The 41-year-old Wisconsin senator claimed to have evidence that the U.S. State Department employed communists. Soon he launched an effort to find them. Later he would seek communists in this country's arts and entertainment industries. Communism was feared because it seemed to be spreading throughout the world, resulting in governments that took away people's freedoms. Communists believed that the government should control economic and political activity.

McCarthyism, as it came to be known, is now seen as a shameful period in American history. Thousands of people who merely held liberal views on such questions as fairness for African Americans or support for poor people were falsely accused of being communists. They lost their jobs; often their lives were ruined. Others survived, but never attained the same status they might have if it weren't for Senator McCarthy.

McCarthy's efforts led to the creation of what was known as the blacklists. These were lists of people who refused to say whether they or anyone they knew had ever been a communist. John Henry Faulk, for example, was a popular radio host and a very wise and funny man from Texas. He was fired because he refused to cooperate with blacklisting.

E.B. White liked to make fun of McCarthy. However, White was devastatingly serious in his critique of McCarthy in a letter to the *New York Herald Tribune*. He wasn't the only one to criticize McCarthy. After several years of intimidation, others started standing up to him. By 1954, McCarthy's power was broken.

McCarthyism left a permanent stain on America's history. But it's possible that there was some benefit. Those who remember McCarthy often insist on respecting rights guaranteed by the U.S. Constitution that McCarthy violated. They include the right to free speech, the right to free association, and the right not to be forced to testify against oneself.

Elwyn had a privileged childhood, living in a large home near New York City in Mount Vernon, New York. He loved animals and the outdoors, although he was prone to allergy attacks. He did well in school, although he was anxious about public speaking. Even as a young boy, he wrote well and prolifically, composing journal entries and letters to relatives as well as prize-winning poetry.

Chapter 2

A WRITER'S BEGINNINGS

Elwyn Brooks White was born on July 11, 1899. His mother, Jessie Hart White, was a homemaker and the daughter of a well-known landscape painter. His father, Samuel Tilly White, was general manager of a piano company. Elwyn was the youngest of six children. His older sisters were Marion, Clara and Lillian. His older brothers were Stanley and Albert. The family lived in a large house in Mount Vernon, just north of New York City.

Mount Vernon is now a densely populated suburb of New York City. In those days it was still rural, with lots of fields, woods and ponds. The children played outside; Elwyn loved to ride his bike and climb trees. His brother, Stanley, taught him to read and write by pointing out letters in newspaper headlines. But Elwyn was shy and did not want to attend school. As he wrote later, "When the time came for me to enter kindergarten, I fought my parents with every ounce of my puny strength. I screamed and carried on. The idea of school terrified me—I wanted to stay home and live peacefully in familiar surroundings."[1]

Elwyn, whose nickname then was "En," lost the battle over going to kindergarten. He attended Public School 2 and did well. He never completely lost his shyness, however. Children in his school were expected to speak in front of assemblies in alphabetical order. Since White begins with W, Elwyn would worry all year about taking his turn in front of the assembly. He was lucky. The year would usually end before his turn came. "I mounted the platform only once in my whole career, but I suffered tortures every day of the school year, thinking about the awesome—if improbable—event,"[2] he wrote later.

Elwyn started writing letters and journal entries when he was about eight. Writing was a challenge, but he found it satisfying. His early letters show that even as a child he had a great eye for detail and a good sense of humor. They also demonstrate what would become a lifelong passion for quality writing and correct spelling. When he was ten years old, Elwyn wrote to his older brother Albert about such events as the passing of Halley's Comet (which appears once every seventy-six years), the state of the family garden, even the strange eating habits of a young nephew. "Wallace Hart (the nephew) still keeps on eating night walkers and live flies and cotton and paper and still looks as well as usual," the letter went. "I guess he takes to his pa for an appetite. I didn't have to ask anybody how to spell appetite cause it was in my spelling lesson."[3]

The White family had plenty of money. They could afford a big house with household help, such as cooks and cleaners. They often spent a month in Maine during the summer, enjoying the outdoors and the cooler weather. But Elwyn's parents were not very social people. Perhaps exaggerating slightly, White wrote that the family never had company for dinner during his childhood.

"For the first eighteen years of my life I never even knew there was such a thing as a dinner party," he wrote. "Nobody got into our house unless he was kinfolks, and even then he had to beat his way in. I might as well have been living in the Rain Forest."4

Samuel White was serious about being a father. He had *Webster's Unabridged Dictionary* mounted on a stand in Albert's room. If his children asked what a word meant, they were sent to the dictionary to look it up. When Elwyn turned 12, Samuel White composed an exuberant letter celebrating his son's birthday. He told his son that he was a lucky boy to have been born in the United States to an educated family. "You have been born in the greatest and best land on the face of the globe under the best government known to men," Samuel White wrote. "Be thankful that you are an American."5

Elwyn was well taken care of and enjoyed many privileges as a child. But he still managed to fill himself with anxiety. "The normal fears and worries of every child were in me developed to a high degree; every day was an awesome prospect," he wrote later. "I was uneasy about practically everything: the uncertainty of the future, the dark of the attic, the panoply and discipline of school, the transitoriness of life, the mystery of the church and God, the frailty of the body, the sadness of the afternoon, the shadow of sex, the distant challenge of love and marriage, the far-off problem of a livelihood. I brooded about them all, lived with them day by day."6

When Elwyn was nine he won the first of his many prizes for writing. The *Woman's Home Companion* gave him an award for a poem he wrote about a mouse. White's lifelong love for animals and the natural world began early. Raising plants and animals fascinated him. Elwyn kept pigeons, dogs, snakes, polliwogs, turtles, lizards, singing birds, chameleons, caterpillars and mice. In Maine he wandered in the woods and canoed through the lakes, happily observing wild animals in their natural surroundings. Elwyn was perhaps more comfortable being alone with animals than being around other children. Many years later, he described a very funny scene in which the mother of Fern, the lead girl character in *Charlotte's Web,* tells the family doctor about how her daughter would rather watch barn animals than play with other children. White might have been drawing on his childhood when he wrote about how Fern, at age eight, preferred animals to people. Describing himself in the third person, Elwyn summed up his interest in animals in an article about his boyhood titled, "A Boy I Knew."

"He always seemed to be under some strange compulsion to assist the processes of incubation and germination, as though without him they might fail and the earth grow old and die," he wrote. "To him a miracle was essentially egg-shaped."[7]

At Mount Vernon High School, Elwyn was the assistant editor of the *Oracle*, the school literary magazine. One of his articles touched on the important news of the day, the growing threat of World War I. He graduated with two scholarships worth $1,000. He should have been happily looking forward to going to Cornell University in upstate New York. But a journal entry from his eighteenth birthday shows the anxiety he felt about his prospects. "My birthday! Eighteen, and still no future. I'd be more contented in prison, for there at least I would know precisely what I had to look forward to,"[8] he wrote.

Despite his gloomy birthday journal entries, he flourished at Cornell. The president of Cornell at the time was Andrew D. White. Since they shared the same last name, Elwyn was given the nickname of Andy. He joined a fraternity and worked on the Cornell *Daily Sun*, one of the few daily college papers in the country at that time. It was more like a regular newspaper because it served both Cornell and the town of Ithaca. The shadow of World War I hung over the campus during his first years at the university. He did not weigh enough to enlist in the army. But he joined the Student Army Training Corps in his second year. Elwyn, who was the historian of his class at Cornell, wrote later about the difficulty of being in college in wartime: "Men studied with one eye on their book and the other on the armed forces of the nation."[9]

Elwyn was sometimes so busy working on the newspaper that he did not delve deeply into his classes at the university. There were however, a few professors who left a lasting impression. One was history professor George Lincoln Burr. At first Burr's class seemed like any other – not particularly interesting. But when Burr spoke, he made the Middle Ages in Europe come alive. Elwyn felt as though he was actually *in* the Middle Ages, when "a few men who still called their souls free were struggling against tyrants and bigots,"[10] he said later in a speech at Cornell. "My chance encounter with George Lincoln Burr was the greatest single thing that ever happened in my life, for he introduced me to a part of myself that I hadn't discovered. I saw, with blinding clarity, how vital it is for man to live in a free society."

Another was William Strunk, an exacting English professor and a stickler for good grammar. Elwyn said Strunk was so forceful and positive that students left class with his demanding sentences firmly imprinted in their minds. Strunk would lean over his desk, grab his coat lapels in his hands, and say, "Omit needless words! Omit needless words! Omit needless words!"[11] Elwyn admired Strunk and kept his advice in mind during his long career as a writer. In 1918, Strunk wrote a short book in which he described what he thought were the most important rules of good writing. Many years later, Elwyn would revise and add to the little book for Macmillan Publishing. Called *The Elements of Style,* it is an important textbook in high school and college English classes. Now in its fourth edition, it is also popular with the general public.

Elwyn also joined the Manuscript Club, an informal meeting on Saturday nights at Professor Martin Sampson's home. Students put unsigned poems or short stories in a box when they arrived at the

William Strunk was one of the Cornell University professors who White remembered fondly. Strunk had high standards for grammatical correctness and clear, concise writing. Many years later, Strunk and White collaborated on a writing manual titled *The Elements of Style.* It was also known simply as Strunk and White's little book.

meeting. In this era, it was legal for professors to serve alcohol to students. So everyone shared a round of shandygaff, which is beer mixed with ginger ale, and took time to visit with one another. Professor Sampson would then read all the manuscripts out loud and everyone would comment on the writing.

Elwyn had terrible allergies–hay fever–all his life. He also had other health problems, such as episodes of dizziness that bothered him for many years. Sometimes it seemed as if he worried too much about his health, or imagined that he was sicker than he really was. One time he wrote in his journal that he was afraid he had tuberculosis. Fortunately, he was wrong. Tuberculosis is a serious, contagious bacterial infection of the lungs that was frequently fatal during his time

Although Elwyn was a good student, he wrote a poem about how he never liked classes on math and economics. The poem displayed what would become his trademark self-critical sense of humor:

In college came a course that dealt
With assets that were frozen.
It was a class I always felt
A tendency to doze in."[12]

Elwyn ended his university career on a high note. He was appointed editor-in-chief of the Cornell *Daily Sun*. In that position, he wrote many articles supporting a plan to put students in charge of the school's honor system. His articles apparently influenced the voters. Both students and professors approved the plan.

During the summers of his last two years at the university, he worked as a camp counselor at Camp Otter in the Canadian province of Ontario. He had a wonderful time taking the boys on canoe trips in the lakes and woods. During his second year, White and another counselor had to evacuate a sick boy on a long nighttime journey through eleven miles of trails and lakes. The boy awoke from a nap too weak to stand and with a strange look in his eyes. The two counselors spent a difficult night carrying the boy over land and paddling across four lakes. "The last two miles were darker than hell's cellar," White wrote in a letter to a girlfriend. "We left the canoe and took turns with the kid, picking our way along. We reached camp just as Mr. Young was putting the fire out–a record trip of a little over two hours."[13] The boy was placed under medical care at Camp Otter. One of Elwyn's duties was to sit with him in an isolation tent as he rambled crazily from the continued fever.

Elwyn had enjoyed a privileged childhood. Then he had succeeded at one of the best universities in the United States. His future should have been secure. But the next few years were anything but easy. Elwyn explored the world of steady work and found it not very much to his liking.

FYInfo

World War I

Europe had been fairly peaceful for a century after the defeat of Napoleon in 1815. But France, Germany, Great Britain and Russia – motivated by years of suspicion and mistrust — planned for possible battles and built large armies and navies. In June, 1914, Archduke Francis Ferdinand, heir to the throne of the Austro-Hungarian Empire, visited Sarajevo. The city was the capital of Bosnia and Herzegovina, part of the empire. A young man from neighboring Serbia, another part of the empire, was resentful of imperial control. He shot and killed the archduke and his wife.

Austria-Hungary declared war on Serbia and asked for backing from Germany. Serbia asked for support from Russia and France. Germany attacked Belgium, which Britain had pledged to protect. By early August, 1914, almost all of Europe was embroiled. In 1915, a German submarine torpedoed the British steamship *Lusitania*. About 1,200 people, including 128 Americans, were killed. In the United States, there was talk of entering the war on the side of France and Britain. But many people felt that Europe was far

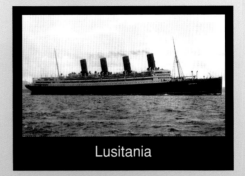

Lusitania

away and that the United States should remain neutral.

Finally in April, 1917, President Woodrow Wilson received a Declaration of War from Congress. American soldiers did not have an immediate impact on the war, but American banks and the U.S. Treasury began supporting and supplying Britain and France. The Russians withdrew from the war after a communist revolution overthrew their government. Finally the Allies—France, Britain, the United States and many other countries—won enough battles to end the war on November 11, 1918.

More than ten million people died and the maps of Europe, Asia and Africa were redrawn. World leaders never wanted to repeat such horror and devastation. They tried to design a lasting peace. But the belief that World War I was "the war to end all wars" turned out to be a false hope. World War II would begin in just twenty-one years.

White had been a good student and the editor in chief of his college newspaper, so it seemed likely that he would be a success in newspapers. But he found newspaper work difficult and sometimes dull. After working for news services and the *Seattle Times*, he eventually found his life-long literary home at the *New Yorker*. The magazine had very high standards and only published the best writing, but it gave him the artistic and creative freedom he needed.

Chapter 3

THE STRUGGLES OF A YOUNG WRITER

New York City attracted White in the same way that it has beckoned to so many young writers before and after his time. After the success he had had at the Cornell *Daily Sun*, going to the city to work for a newspaper seemed logical. His friends were working at some of the many New York daily newspapers. He soon found a job as a reporter and an editor for the United Press news service. News services, such as the United Press, supply articles to newspapers, especially smaller papers that cannot afford to have reporters at every national news event. Though he didn't like the job, White found he could edit the articles and handle the deskwork fairly well. But his first assignment was to cover the funeral of U.S. Senator Philander C. Knox in Philadelphia. He took the wrong train and arrived late. He promptly quit and began looking for something else. He found another job writing press releases at the American Legion News Service. Press releases are articles produced by businesses and other organizations in hopes that newspaper editors will print them. He didn't like this job either.

White was a writer, but he wanted to write poetry and essays and articles that were interesting to him. He disliked the idea of having to sit at a desk and be required to churn out prose on boring topics. In a letter to a friend, he joked that his work in public relations was at least providing jobs for other people. "I am the person who furnishes the material that keeps the janitors employed," he wrote. "If it wasn't for me there would be thousands of janitors out of work in New York City. I write the stories, the city editors brush 'em out on to the floor, and the janitors sweep 'em up."[1]

White spent his evenings writing the sort of poetry and other pieces that interested him. He had a few items published in local newspapers. But he was restless and began reconsidering the idea of going straight into the world of full-time work. He and a friend from Cornell, Howard Cushman, decided to go on a long cross-country trip. They packed their things into White's Model T Ford roadster and set off on their adventure. They had little money, and planned to support themselves by selling articles about their trip to newspapers.

The pair drove slowly across the country, stopping to visit friends, see the sights, and sometimes camp in whatever park or ugly old campground they could find. They watched horse races in Kentucky, visited universities, and worked as ranch hands in Montana. At times they were so low on money they sold their possessions, including a typewriter. But they still managed to enjoy themselves and take in the vastness and the beauty of the American West.

After months of traveling, they wound up in Seattle, Washington. White decided to try his hand at journalism once again. In September, 1922, he started working as a reporter at the *Seattle Times*. He lasted longer there than he had at other writing jobs, but continued to find newspaper work difficult.

"Johns (the city editor) soon realized that in me he had a special problem. Although punctual and neat, I didn't know the meaning of the word, 'indictment' and was unable to hear anything over the telephone,"[2] White wrote later.

In those days, reporters would call their stories into the newsroom, and people at the paper were expected to type the story quickly as the reporter spoke over the telephone. But the reporters, or "legmen," as they were called, perhaps concerned about misunderstandings over the sometimes scratchy telephones, would insist on spelling words out using their own mysterious system. They would say, "B for Boston," and "C for Chicago," until White became so confused he would lose the thread of the story. He particularly hated covering crime stories, which were probably as important to newspaper editors then as they are today.

He did better when he was assigned to write feature articles. Later he was given a column, where he could write jokes and poems in his matchless fashion. It wasn't enough. The *Seattle Times* fired White on June 19, 1923. The editors knew he was talented, but they might have realized that he was more of an artist and a writer than a newspaperman.

White decided to wander a little more before looking for another job. He used his savings to buy a ticket on a cruise ship going to Alaska. He traveled in style–first class–to Skagway in southern Alaska. Near the end of the voyage, he asked the captain for a job. The captain said no and White sadly disembarked in Skagway. But after he had sat on the dock for a few minutes, the daughter of one of the ship's owners came running out to offer him a job on the ship. Quickly he was back on board, living the hard life of a crew member instead of the easy life of a first-class passenger.

The ship soon hit three days of terrible weather. Many of the passengers became extremely seasick. White felt fine. He worked hard taking care of the sick and serving food to those who could still eat. Later he wrote that surviving the storm so well made him feel much better about being young and not knowing what to do with himself. "Youth is almost always a time of deep trouble—of the mind, the heart, the flesh. And as a youth I think I managed to heap myself with more than my share," White wrote in an article. "It took an upheaval of the elements and a job at the lowest level to give me the relief I craved."[3]

The ship returned to Seattle and White returned to New York. It would still be a few years before he found his calling. He was a little more grown up now and ready to continue to pursue his career as a writer.

FYInfo

The Roaring Twenties

The United States emerged from World War I as a world power. There was a brief economic depression from 1920 to 1921, but in general the following years were so prosperous that the decade became known as the Roaring Twenties. The country had access to more markets. Industrialization – especially the development of the automobile companies — led to continued economic growth. Henry Ford developed the assembly line as an efficient way to mass-produce cars. He also promoted the concept of paying workers enough so that they could afford to buy the same cars they were producing. The stock market, in which people could increase their wealth by investing their savings in profitable businesses, rose rapidly.

The decade saw profound cultural changes. Conservative American society, in which people were expected to go to church every Sunday and women always covered their bodies with long dresses, gave way to new experiments and freedoms. Women wore makeup and shorter dresses. Jazz, an exciting new musical form developed by African Americans in

Henry Ford

the south, became popular throughout the country. The government imposed a ban on alcohol known as Prohibition, but that only led to the secret — and extremely popular — dance and drinking clubs known as the speakeasies.

The Twenties were also a decade of contradiction. While many people became very wealthy, other workers toiled and remained in extreme poverty. However, the majority of Americans saw unprecedented freedoms and prosperity in the 1920s. They thought it would last forever. Few considered the fast growth of the uncontrolled stock market could cause any problems. But it did. It all came crashing down when the stock market collapsed in late 1929. That led to the Great Depression.

James Thurber (shown here on the right) was a humorist and writer searching for an outlet when he met E.B. White. Despite their differences, the two worked together and White helped Thurber see how good his own cartoon drawings were. Thurber went on to become one of America's most famous writers and humorists, perhaps best known for the short story, "The Secret Life of Walter Mitty."

Chapter 4

FINDING SUCCESS IN NEW YORK CITY

Something new was happening in New York City when White returned. Harold Ross, a former newspaperman, started a new magazine called *The New Yorker* in 1925. He had a vision of a cutting-edge publication that would offer writing better than any of the other magazines available. It had wonderful cartoons and lots of jokes. White began submitting work to the magazine and Ross published it. White, who had drifted from job to job since graduating from Cornell, finally found a place he liked to work.

Ross was undoubtedly the driving force behind *The New Yorker,* which would eventually grow into an American treasure. The history of the magazine is filled with references to White. White's singular writing style and his great sense of humor helped to make the magazine special in its early days.

White also formed a somewhat mysterious partnership with James Thurber, who went on to become a famous humorist. Where White was understated and reserved, Thurber was wild and wacky. The two shared an office for many years and their contradictory personalities often seemed to bring out the best in each other. Thurber had a light and funny artistic style that was not appreciated at first. He had a habit of scribbling his funny little drawings and throwing them on the floor.

White and Thurber decided to write a book titled *Is Sex Necessary?* It was a spoof on the serious books on sex that were being published at the time. White scooped some of Thurber's drawings off the floor, and suggested Thurber pencil a few more. White painstakingly inked over the pencil lines and presented Thurber's drawings as the illustrations for their book. The editor of the book at first hesitated because Thurber was not known as an illustrator, but he decided to trust White's judgment. The book was a success and helped launch Thurber's career.

White wrote articles, short stories and poetry for *The New Yorker*. He edited other writers' work. He helped dream up captions for the cartoons that would eventually become one of the magazine's most famous features. He was perhaps best known for a quirky little feature called newsbreaks. These were excerpts from other newspapers and magazines. These excerpts often had mistakes or some other oddity, followed by White's cheeky comment. White started writing newsbreaks for the *New Yorker* in 1926. His other work at the magazine ebbed and flowed over the next fifty years, but he continued to write newsbreaks. "I still regard newsbreaks as the thing I came to earth for,"[1] White said. Readers loved the feature, and they sent hundreds of clippings of funny stories or mistakes for the *New Yorker* to consider.

Newsbreaks were never signed, so it is difficult to say which ones White wrote. One that appeared in the Feb. 18, 1939 edition could well have been one of his. It featured a paragraph from the Cincinnati Symphony Orchestra program that stated, "When he was twenty years of age he went to London and studied the violin. For five years thereafter he was bandmaster at the County Lunatic Asylum."[2] The comment that followed was, "Next time he'll stay home, maybe."[3] The next week's newsbreaks included a headline from the *Poughkeepsie Star & Enterprise* that proclaimed "TWO PERSONS HURT IN ROUTE 9-D CRASH – Peekskill Woman Suffers Consciousness."[4] The observation that followed was, "It's a cross many of us have to bear."[5] It's poking fun at the newspaper's mistake in saying that the woman suffers from *consciousness* instead of *unconsciousness*.

At *The New Yorker* White had not only found a job he enjoyed and was good at, he also met Katharine Angell. She was a brilliant young graduate of Bryn Mawr College who had been hired as a manuscript reader at the magazine. She had an eye for editing and seeing potential in writers, and was good at coaxing out their best work. She eventually became fiction editor. White, who had always been shy around women, wrote poems to Katharine. She was taken with him and the two fell in love. They were married in November, 1929. Their only son, Joel McCoun White, was born on December 21, 1930.

White and Katharine both had good jobs at *The New Yorker.* White also had income from *Is Sex Necessary?* and *The Lady is Cold*, his first book of poetry published in 1929. While many people lost their jobs and their savings in the Great Depression, the Whites did not suffer financially. But economic problems ravaged all around them. Franklin Delano Roosevelt, a Democrat who promised to use the government in unprecedented ways to get the economy back on its feet, was elected president in 1933. White, who by then was an increasingly popular writer and poet, was perhaps more harshly criticized at that time than at any other point in his career. *Fortune* magazine published a long article saying that the *New Yorker* should report more aggressively on the economy and support efforts to end the suffering. The article singled out White in particular, saying he

Katharine Angell White was an editor at the *New Yorker* and White's life-long soul mate. She wrote occasional essays on gardening for the *New Yorker.* Toward the end of her life, she was plagued with health problems but she was still devoted to the gardens on their farm in Maine. *The New York Times* called *Onward and Upward in the Garden,* the collection of her gardening articles White published after her death in 1977, "a bouquet, the final blooming of an extraordinary sensibility."

was more concerned with pet fish and his own dogs than hungry people in the streets. The criticism was no doubt painful, but White continued to write the way he wanted to. He never worried too much about what other people were saying about him.

White enjoyed New York City and *The New Yorker*, but he was still a country boy at heart. He missed the rural life. By 1938 he and Katharine were able to buy a small farm on the coastline near North Brooklin, Maine. White continued to work for *The New Yorker*, but he also began writing long essays for *Harper's* magazine. In those articles, White ranged over a wide variety of topics, from the birth of lambs on his farm to international politics. The articles told great stories and they were funny. In a story on his first season as midwife to his pregnant ewes, he wrote:

> At first, birth strikes one as the supreme example of bad planning—a thoroughly mismanaged and ill-advised functional process, something thought up by a dirty-minded fiend. It appears cluttery, haphazard. But after you have been mixed up with it for a while, have spent nights squatting beneath a smoky lantern in a cold horse stall helping a weak lamb whose mother fails to own it; after you have grown accustomed to the odd trappings and byproducts of mammalian reproduction and seen how marvelously they contribute to the finished product; after you have broken down an animal's reserve and have identified yourself with her and no longer pull your punches, then this strange phenomenon of birth becomes an absorbingly lustrous occasion, full of subdued emotions, like a great play, an occasion for which you unthinkingly give up any other occupation that might be demanding your attention. I've never before in my life put in such a month as this past

month has been—a period of pure creation, vicarious in its nature, but extraordinarily moving.[6]

Perhaps White was sometimes more concerned with animals than people. He was very much his own person and he alone decided what would be the focus of his preoccupations.

As the 1930s continued, the depression spread around the world. White foresaw the dangers of new fascist governments that were coming to power and promising superiority over other countries. Fascism is a political system that promises order and control, but takes away freedoms. It also relies on wars to win support from the population. This dangerous belief system, which ended up leading to World War II, was spreading throughout the world. Adolf Hitler came to power in Germany. General Francisco Franco won a war for power over the elected government of Spain. Imperial Japan was attacking its neighbors. White saw the evil of these dictators perhaps more clearly than other writers.

Anne Morrow Lindbergh was a widely admired writer, the wife of the famous pilot Charles Lindbergh (the first man to fly alone across the Atlantic Ocean), and the mother of a child who had been kidnapped and brutally murdered. She wrote a book called *The Wave of the Future*. The book argued against the United States going to war against Hitler. It said that the German people had elected Hitler and that the United States should not oppose him when his armies attacked his neighbors. White wrote a long, detailed, and clearly argued review of the book. "The fascist ideal," he wrote, "however great the misery which released it and however impressive the self-denial and the burning courage which promote it, does not hold the seed of a better order, but a worse one...It stank in the time of Christ and it stinks today..."[7]

Though White increasingly wrote about international events, he continued to believe that it was at times right to focus on life at home. In 1941 he wrote, "Countries are ransacked, valleys drenched with blood. Though it seems untimely I still publish my belief in the egg, the contents of the egg, the warm coal, and the necessity of pursuing whatever fire delights and sustains you."[8]

This picture shows the USS Arizona Memorial in Pearl Harbor, Hawaii. The United States entered World War II after the Japanese attacked Pearl Harbor. White was profoundly affected by the violence of World War II. It led him to advocate for a world government that would prevent future wars. Though he never succeeded in persuading world leaders to form a world government, he did have hopes for the United Nations.

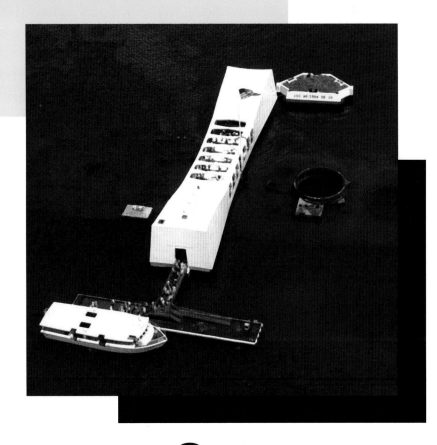

Chapter 4 FINDING SUCCESS IN NEW YORK CITY

The United States declared war after Japan attacked the U.S. naval base at Pearl Harbor in Hawaii on December 7, 1941. White returned to *The New Yorker* full-time to help because so many writers had joined the military. During World War II, White turned his attention to finding a way to stop future wars. He wrote untiringly, and with great creativity and genius, about the need for a world government. Many people, including his editor, Harold Ross, told him it was impractical. Countries would never agree to a single government. But White—in hindsight quite wisely—believed a world government was the only way to prevent future wars. He wrote about the importance of world government in a way that was easy to understand and convincing to the ordinary person. He once compared the existing system of independent countries to a baseball game.

"It is as though eighteen ball players went out on a diamond, each having evolved his own policy regarding the bat, the ball, the glove, and the bases," he wrote. "One player's policy is to run directly from first to third without bothering with second. Another secretly resolves to conceal a bat in his shirt and rap the pitcher over the head with it. Another decides to keep tossing the ball up in the air and catching it, in solitary glee. It doesn't make for an orderly ball game, yet it is the system by which nations live..."[9]

White became more famous after his essays from *Harper's* were published in a book titled *One Man's Meat*. He was becoming well known as an essayist, a humorist, and a commentator. But the three books that would eventually make him a household name lay ahead.

FYInfo

The United Nations

In the early days of World War II, President Franklin Roosevelt and English Prime Minister Winston Churchill agreed that the nations of the world needed to form a strong international organization that would prevent future wars. The League of Nations had been formed after World War I, but it was a weak grouping and failed to prevent World War II.

A series of meetings was held during and after World War II to form the new international peacekeeping organization, dubbed the United Nations by President Roosevelt. Representatives of 50 nations met in San Francisco, California, in April of 1945 to draw up the United Nations charter, or constitution. The United Nations officially came into existence on Oct. 24, 1945.

E.B. White thought the world needed a government, not an organization, but he was still hopeful that the United Nations would succeed in preventing future wars. He traveled to the San Francisco conference. "The rich and ribald spectacle of these pre-Conference hours neither conceals nor removes the sense of destiny and the sense of obligation which haunt the citadel," he wrote. "The accusing eye of millions of

President Roosevelt

homesick young soldiers, the hungry gaze of millions of famished children, are trained on this hill tonight. Theirs is a fixed stare, which no one can evade. It waits for every delegate at the bottom of his glass."[1]

The United Nations has certainly not been able to prevent all wars. But there has not been another world war since it was founded. It has helped to resolve many conflicts inside countries and between countries. It has also established organizations to aid children, refugees and other needy people. United Nations organizations have won the Nobel Peace Prize five times. The most recent award came in 2001, with the United Nations itself sharing the prize with Secretary General Kofi Annan.

E.B. White was once criticized for taking too much interest in animals, especially his dog Minnie. But he was fascinated with animals all his life and that fascination helped him write his three great children's books, *Stuart Little, Charlotte's Web,* and *The Trumpet of the Swan.* Ironically, a leading librarian of the time urged him not to publish *Stuart Little,* saying the book was too fantastic, or unlikely. But he went ahead and it became one of the world's most popular children's books.

Chapter 5

THE INSPIRATION FOR
STUART LITTLE

There is little indication that White wanted to become one of the greatest children's book writers this country has ever produced. He simply had many nieces and nephews who loved to hear stories. Televisions were not so common in those days and there weren't as many children's books as there are today. Adults would often make up stories to tell children at bedtime. White found he could not think up stories at the spur of the moment. So he sat down and wrote a series of tales about a tiny mouse-child named Stuart Little.

He was feeling ill in 1945. He was afraid that he was going to leave very little money for his family to live on if he died. He decided to turn the episodes about Stuart Little into a children's novel. His publisher, Harper & Row, eagerly agreed to publish the book. But in the process, the publisher decided to let Anne Carroll Moore, a very influential librarian and children's book critic, review the galleys, or early editions. Moore, for many years the children's librarian at the New York City Public Library, had urged White to write for children. A book of her articles begins by saying, "she was a discoverer and a proclaimer, a celebrant of originality."[1]

But Moore did not like White's originality. She disliked the book so much she urged him not to publish it, writing that she thought the book would be an "embarrassment" to him. Moore wrote "one of the most difficult letters I have ever attempted" to White. She told him, "After the first chapter I feel the story getting more and more out of hand, the invention becoming labored and Stuart himself staggering out of scale."[2] The chapter in which Stuart works as a substitute teacher for one day especially drew her disdain. That's ironic, because many children find that chapter to be extremely funny.

When Stuart takes over the class, the students tell him they usually study spelling. "Well," the mouse-child says, "a misspelled word is an abomination in the sight of everyone. I consider it a very fine thing to spell words correctly and I strongly urge every one of you to buy a Webster's Collegiate Dictionary and consult it whenever in doubt. So much for spelling. What's next?"[3] The children in Stuart's class are delighted that they don't have to study spelling, and readers of the book find the scene just as delightful.

White considered the suggestion that he withdraw the book from publication but decided to ignore it. "I was shook up by the letter but not deflected," White wrote later. "I learned two things from the experience of writing *Stuart Little*: that a writer's nose is his best guide, and that children can sail easily over the fence that separates reality from make-believe. They go over it like little springboks. A fence that can throw a librarian is nothing to a child."[4] *Stuart Little* went on to become a huge best-seller. It has been translated into many languages and also made into a very popular movie.

One of the amazing aspects of White's career is that he often worked just as hard as a farmer as he did as a writer. During World War II the government required him to fill out a description of his work. He wrote a funny article describing his efforts to explain his life as a writer and a farmer on a government form that did not really allow for such a mix of professions. He joked in the article, "Physically I am better suited for writing than farming, because farming takes great strength and endurance. Intellectually I am better suited for farming than writing."[5]

One day White was working on his farm, feeding the pigs and the geese. He had an idea about a spider that saves the life of a pig on the way to the butcher. He developed the idea into *Charlotte's Web*, perhaps his most famous story. The main characters are Wilbur the pig, Charlotte the spider, and Fern, the girl who understands the animals' barnyard conversations. Fern was not introduced at the beginning of the book in White's first draft. But White thought about the plot for a while and then rewrote the book to give Fern a more important role. He began the story in a new, particularly gripping way: "'Where's Pa going with that ax?' said Fern to her mother as they were setting the table for breakfast."[6] That opening line sets the tone for an unforgettable book that tells the story of how Charlotte saves Wilbur by writing words in her web. Since Charlotte was a spider, she died after she laid her eggs. But Wilbur lived on to enjoy the presence of Charlotte's children, her grandchildren, and successive generations.

White had no idea how successful the book would be. When he signed the contract for the book in 1952, he agreed that Harper & Row should not pay him more than $7,500 a year in royalties, pushing any excess into the next year's payment. This was commonly done to avoid problems with a writer owing too much money in taxes. But *Charlotte's Web* was so profitable that the contract provision was perhaps a mistake. When White finally withdrew the excess royalty fees in 1979, the total was more than half a million dollars!

As White and Katharine grew older, they were both dealing with increasingly severe health problems. White's stomach had bothered him off and on all his life. Katharine suffered from heart trouble and back trouble, and often needed the care of a nurse at home. White had always earned a good living from his writing for *The New Yorker* and his many books, but the inspiration for his last children's book—*The Trumpet of the Swan*—came from concerns about the high cost of nursing care. White wrote, "It took a lot of gall to write it, as I have never in my life laid eyes on a Trumpeter Swan, either in or out of captivity. But I'll tackle anything in a pinch, and I began to feel the pinch more than a year ago when I looked around and discovered that my house was full of day nurses and night nurses at $28 per day."[7]

In *The Trumpet of the Swan*, White invented a baby swan, or cygnet, called Louis, who was born without a voice. His father sees that the love of Louis's life will never pay any attention to Louis because he cannot speak. Against his better judgment, he flies to Billings, Montana, breaks into a music store and steals a trumpet for his voiceless son. Through many twists and turns, Louis spends the rest of the book learning to read and write, earning enough money to pay back the store. He finally wins the affection of his sweetheart.

Once again, White based his fantasy in reality. He carefully researched details about trumpeter swans' migration patterns and other habits. A friend in Philadelphia visited the Philadelphia Zoo and gave White an extensive report on the trumpeter swans there. White also drew on his familiarity with the geese at his farm.

Although *The Trumpet of the Swan* was never as popular as *Stuart Little* and *Charlotte's Web*, it was beautifully written and well-received. John Updike, another famous writer, praised it. "White never forgets that he is telling about serious matters: the overcoming of a handicap, and the joys of music, and the need for creatures to find a mate, and the survival of a beautiful species of swan,"[8] Updike wrote.

Composer Benjamin Lee noted the unusual role of music in the story and created a special musical composition based on *The Trumpet of the Swan*. The Philadelphia Orchestra gave the world premiere of the music in 1972, along with a shortened version of the story.

Katharine White died in 1977 at the age of 84. White mourned her passing and paid tribute to her by publishing a collection of her articles on gardening, *Onward and Upward in the Garden*. White lived until 1985, enjoying his farm in Maine and writing numerous letters to friends and readers. When he died on October 1 of Alzheimer's Disease at the age of 86, the *New York Times* heralded him as "one of the nation's most precious literary resources."[9]

One of E.B. White's many eccentricities was that he disagreed with the typical practice of paying an actor to read a book for the recorded book market. He thought books should be read clearly and with good pronunciation. But he did not believe they should be read too dramatically. As a result, one can still hear White's voice by listening to his recorded versions of *The Trumpet of the Swan* or *Charlotte's Web*.

White also lives on each and every day that someone curls up in bed with one of his wonderful books, and thinks, laughs, and marvels at his style and creativity.

FYInfo

Henry David Thoreau

In the 1960s, many Americans felt the war the U.S. government was waging in Vietnam was wrong. They also became more aware of the injustice of the second-class treatment received by African Americans and other minorities in the United States. They wondered how to bring fair treatment to minority groups in their own country and peace to Vietnam. Many turned to a nineteenth century American writer and philosopher, Henry David Thoreau.

Thoreau was born in 1817 and graduated from Harvard University. In 1845 he built a crude cabin on the shores of Walden Pond near Concord, Massachusetts, and lived there for two years. He wanted to live simply and take time to write and observe nature. His book, *Walden; or a Life in the Woods* is an enduring classic about the beauty of nature and living without so much concern about money. E.B. White considered *Walden* the most important book he ever read. "It is not the best book I ever encountered, perhaps, but is for me the handiest, and I keep it about me in much the same way one carries a handkerchief—for relief in moments of defluxion and despair,"[1] he wrote.

Henry David Thoreau

In 1846 Thoreau went to jail rather than pay a tax used to pay for war against Mexico. He wrote an essay on civil disobedience, *Resistance to a Civil Government*. It inspired Mohandas Gandhi, who led the people of India in non-violent rebellion against the colonial powers of England. It also inspired Martin Luther King Jr. and others who worked in the civil rights movement to provide equal rights to all Americans.

Thoreau died in 1862, but he became very important to White and other Americans years after his death. An illustrated collection of his writings, chosen especially for children, was published in 1967 and subtitled *A Man for Our Time*. Today, Walden Pond remains an historic place where people go to remember Henry David Thoreau.

CHRONOLOGY

1899 Born in Mount Vernon, N.Y., on July 11

1909 Wins prize for writing a poem about a mouse

1917 Graduates from Mount Vernon High School and enters Cornell University

1921 Graduates from Cornell; works for the United Press in York City

1922 Drives across the United States with his friend, Howard Cushman

1926 Joins the *New Yorker* staff

1929 Marries Katharine Angell

1930 Joel McCoun White, his only child, is born on December 21

1933 Buys a farm in North Brooklin, Maine, which is eventually immortalized in *Charlotte's Web*

1945 Publishes *Stuart Little*

1952 Publishes *Charlotte's Web*

1957 Moves permanently to his farm in Maine, after many years of going back and forth between the farm and New York City

1963 Is awarded the Presidential Medal of Freedom by President John F. Kennedy

1970 Publishes *The Trumpet of the Swan,* wins the Laura Ingalls Wilder prize

1973 *Charlotte's Web*, the movie, is released; *The Trumpet of the Swan* wins the William Allen White Children's Book Award and the Sequoyah Children's Book Award

1977 Katharine White dies at the age of 84

1978 Awarded a special Pulitzer Prize for his body of work

1985 Dies on October 1

1999 Film version of *Stuart Little* becomes extremely popular, and is followed by a sequel in 2002

2003 Release of the film *Charlotte's Web II: Wilbur's Great Adventure* testifies to the continuing popularity of White's book

2004 *The Elements of Style*, 4th Edition, ranks in the top 500 of all books sold by Amazon.com

TIMELINE IN HISTORY

1857 The U.S. Supreme Court upholds slavery in the *Dred Scott* decision.

1861 The Civil War begins after southern states secede and form the Confederate States of America.

1865 The Civil War ends; President Abraham Lincoln, who led the Union to victory, is assassinated.

1873 The *New York Daily Graphic*, the first illustrated daily newspaper, begins publication.

1890 As wars against the Native Americans continue, 200 Sioux are massacred at Wounded Knee, South Dakota.

1903 Orville and Wilbur Wright fly the first mechanically propelled airplane near Kitty Hawk, North Carolina.

1917 The United States declares war on Germany and enters World War I.

1920 Women in the United States win the right to vote.

1929 The Great Depression begins with the crash of the stock market.

1933 Franklin D. Roosevelt is elected president and begins to combat the Depression with many government programs.

1939 Germany begins World War II by invading Poland.

1941 The United States enters World War II after the Japanese attack Pearl Harbor.

1945 Harry S Truman becomes president after President Roosevelt dies in office; the United States drops atomic bombs on Hiroshima and Nagasaki.

1954 The United States Senate censures Senator Joseph McCarthy, who has been leading an investigation of communist beliefs among artists, government employees, writers, and others.

1960 The Civil Rights movement heats up as people across the South participate in sit-ins to protest segregation.

1963 President John F. Kennedy is assassinated in Dallas, Texas.

1968 Presidential candidate Robert F. Kennedy and civil rights leader Martin Luther King, Jr. are assassinated.

1974 President Richard Nixon resigns amid the Watergate scandal.

1975 The Vietnam War ends.

1980 The United States boycotts the Olympics to protest the Soviet Union's invasion of Afghanistan.

1991 President George Bush sends soldiers to the Persian Gulf to free Kuwait from Iraqi occupation.

1995 A terror bombing in Oklahoma City kills 168 people.

2001 Terrorists hijack three airplanes and crash them into the Pentagon outside Washington D.C., and the World Trade Center towers in New York City; a fourth hijacked plane crashes in rural Pennsylvania.

2003 President George W. Bush sends troops to invade Iraq and remove the government of Saddam Hussein.

2004 United States cyclist Lance Armstrong wins his sixth consecutive Tour de France.

CHAPTER NOTES

Chapter 1
Baby Spiders on the Dresser

1. Scott Elledge, *E. B. White: A Biography* (New York: W. W. Norton & Company, 1984), p. 294.

Chapter 2
A Writer's Beginnings

1. Dorothy Lobrano Guth, *Letters of E. B. White* (New York: Harper & Row, 1976), pp. 7-8.

2. Ibid., p. 8.

3. Ibid., p. 12.

4. Ibid., p. 514.

5. Scott Elledge, *E. B. White: A Biography* (New York: W. W. Norton & Company, 1984), p. 4.

6. Dorothy Lobrano Guth, *Letters of E. B. White* (New York: Harper & Row, 1976), p. 1.

7. Scott Elledge, *E. B. White: A Biography* (New York: W. W. Norton & Company, 1984), p. 25.

8. E. B. White, *One Man's Meat* (New York: Harper & Row, 1938), p. 111.

9. Scott Elledge, *E. B. White: A Biography* (New York: W. W. Norton & Company, 1984), p. 51.

10. Ibid., p. 58.

11. William Strunk Jr. & E. B. White, *Elements of Style*, 4th edition (Needham Heights, Massachusetts: Allyn and Bacon, 2000), p. xv.

12. E. B. White, *The Fox of Peapack* (New York: Harper & Brothers, 1928), p. 9.

13. Dorothy Lobrano Guth, *Letters of E. B. White* (New York: Harper & Row, 1976), p. 22.

Chapter 3
The Struggles of a Young Writer

1. Dorothy Lobrano Guth, *Letters of E. B. White* (New York: Harper & Row, 1976), p. 28.

2. E. B. White, *The Second Tree from the Corner* (New York: Harper & Brothers, 1935), p. 11.

3. E. B. White, *The Points of My Compass* (New York: Harper & Row, 1954), p. 240.

Chapter 4
Finding Success in New York

1. Ben Yagoda, *About Town: The New Yorker and the World It Made* (New York: Scribner, 2000), p. 49.

2. *The New Yorker*, Feb. 18, 1939.

3. Ibid.

4. *The New Yorker*, Feb. 25, 1939.

5. Ibid.

6. E. B. White, *One Man's Meat* (New York: Harper & Row, 1938), p. 156.

7. Ibid., p. 206.

8. Ibid., p. 237.

9. E. B. White, *The Wild Flag* (Cambridge, Massachusetts: The Riverside Press, 1943), p. 25.

FYI: United Nations

1. Scott Elledge, *E. B. White: A Biography* (New York: W. W. Norton & Company, 1984), p. 244.

Chapter 5
The Inspiration for *Stuart Little*

1. Anne Carroll Moore, *My Roads to Childhood: Views and Reviews of Children's Books* (Boston: The Horn Book, Inc., 1961), p. x.

2. Frances Clark Sayers, *Anne Carroll Moore* (New York: Antheneum, 1972), p. 244.

3. E. B. White, *Stuart Little* (New York: Harper & Row, 1945), p. 90.

4. Scott Elledge, *E. B. White: A Biography* (New York: W. W. Norton & Company, 1984), p. 263.

5. E. B. White, *One Man's Meat* (New York: Harper & Row, 1938), p. 293.

6. E. B. White, *Charlotte's Web* (New York: Harper & Row, 1945), p. 1.

7. Dorothy Lobrano Guth, *Letters of E. B. White* (New York: Harper & Row, 1976), p. 605.

8. John Updike, *Picked-up Pieces* (New York: Alfred E. Knopf, Inc., 1966), p. 43.

9. *New York Times*, Oct. 2, 1985.

FYI: Henry David Thoreau

1. E. B. White, *Writings from the New Yorker 1925-1976* (New York: Harper Collins Publishers, 1990), p. 45.

FURTHER READING

For Young Adults

Gherman, Beverly. *E. B. White: Some Writer!* New York: Atheneum, 1992.

Litwin, Laura Baskes. *E. B. White: Beyond Charlotte's Web and Stuart Little*. Berkeley Heights, New Jersey: Enslow Publishers, 2003.

Tingum, Janice. *E.B. White: Elements of a Writer*. Minneapolis, Minnesota: Lerner Books, 1995.

White, E.B. *Charlotte's Web*. New York: Harper & Row, 1952.

White, E.B. *Stuart Little*. New York: Harper & Row, 1945.

White, E.B. *The Trumpet of the Swan*. New York: Harper & Row, 1970.

Works Consulted

Elledge, Scott. *E.B. White: A Biography*. New York: W.W. Norton & Company, 1984.

Guth, Dorothy Lobrano, editor. *Letters of E.B. White*. New York: Harper & Row, 1976.

Mitgang, Herbert. "E.B. White, Essayist, Stylist, Dies." *The New York Times*, Oct. 2, 1985.

Moore, Anne Carroll. *My Roads to Childhood: Views and Reviews of Children's Books*. Boston: The Horn Book, Inc., 1961.

Sayers, Frances Clarke. *Anne Carroll Moore*. New York: Atheneum, 1972.

Strunk, William Jr. and White, E.B. *The Elements of Style*, 4th edition. Needham Heights, Massachusetts: Allyn and Bacon, 2000.

Updike, John. *Picked-up Pieces*. New York: Alfred E. Knopf, Inc., 1966.

White, E.B. *Every Day is Saturday*. New York: Harper & Brothers, 1934.

White, E.B. *The Fox of Peapack*. New York: Harper & Brothers, 1928.

White, E.B. *The Lady is Cold*. New York: Harper and Brothers, 1929.

White, E.B. *The Letters of E.B. White*. New York: Harper & Row, 1976.

White, E.B. *One Man's Meat*. New York: Harper & Row, 1938.

White, E.B. *Poems & Sketches of E.B. White*. New York: Harper & Row, 1925.

White, E.B. *The Points of My Compass*. New York: Harper & Row, 1954.

White, E.B. *Quo Vadimus? Or The Case for the Bicycle*. New York: Grosset & Dunlap, 1927.

White, E.B. *The Second Tree from the Corner*. New York: Harper & Brothers, 1935.

White, E.B. *The Wild Flag*. Cambridge, Mass.: The Riverside Press, 1943.

White, E.B. *Writings from the New Yorker: 1925-1976*. New York: HarperCollins Publishers, 1990.

Yagoda, Ben. *About Town: The New Yorker and the World It Made*. New York: Scribner, 2000.

On the Internet

E.B. White Official Web Page
http://www.ebwhitebooks.com

GLOSSSARY

abomination (uh-bah-mi-NAY-shun)
something terrible or very strange

bigot (BIG-uht)
person who holds prejudiced views toward other people

citadel (SIT-uh-dell)
a fortress that overlooks a city

communism (KOM-you-nism)
Belief that the government should control the nation's economy in order to make sure everyone is treated fairly

compulsion (com-PUL-shun)
impulse to do something

depression (dee-PRESH-un)
period when economic activity falls and people lose jobs

dictator (dic-TAY-tor)
ruler having absolute power, rather than a democratically elected leader

economic (eh-kuh-NOM-ic)
having to do with money.

enlist (ehn-LIST)
sign up for something, usually military service

exuberant (ex-OOH-ber-ant)
characterized by excitement and wildness

fascism (FA-shism)
system of beliefs that holds a certain race or country above others and believes that the government should control political activity and promote militarism

fiend (FEEND)
the devil or a wicked person

frailty (FRALE-tee)
characteristic of being weak

germination (jur-mi-NAY-shun)
process through which a seed begins growing into a plant

indictment (in-DYET-mint)
formal accusation

incubation (in-cu-BAY-shun)
process of warming an egg so that it hatches

ironic (eye-RAHN-ick)
kind of humor or writing that comes from something being unexpected

lustrous (LUSS-truss)
shiny

neutral (NOO-tral)
not taking sides in a conflict

panoply (PAN-uh-plee)
impressively wide variety of things within a certain category

phenomenon (fen-NAH-me-nun)
unusual occurrence

rappel (ruh-PELL)
use a rope to climb down.

ribald (RYE-bald)
uncontrolled, possibly crude

rural (RUHR-uhl)
having to do with the countryside away from a city

scholarship (SKAHL-ur-ship)
money to pay for education; achievements of a scholar

transitoriness (trans-it-TOR-ee-ness)
characteristic of being temporary

tyrant (TIE-rant)
person who rules cruelly and absolutely

Unitarian (you-ni-TEAR-ee-an)
member of a religion that emphasizes individual freedom of belief and social service

vicarious (vie-KARE-ee-ous)
experienced through the participation of another person

INDEX